# VISIONS AND DREAMS UNVEILED

## SHERREL HENDRIX

Bloomington, IN  Milton Keynes, UK

authorHOUSE®

*AuthorHouse*™
*1663 Liberty Drive, Suite 200*
*Bloomington, IN 47403*
*www.authorhouse.com*
*Phone: 1-800-839-8640*

*AuthorHouse*™ *UK Ltd.*
*500 Avebury Boulevard*
*Central Milton Keynes, MK9 2BE*
*www.authorhouse.co.uk*
*Phone: 08001974150*

*First published by AuthorHouse    3/13/2007*

*ISBN: 978-1-4259-4439-1 (sc)*

*Printed in the United States of America*
*Bloomington, Indiana*

*This book is printed on acid-free paper.*

# INTRODUCTION

On the second Sunday in February of 1997, I went to church as usual. The weather was unusually humid, and warm for that time of the year. I felt a little discouraged. I really wanted the Lord to show and direct me in a path that was pleasing to Him.

In the middle of church service, Pastor Hood asked if we would close our eyes for a minute of silent prayer. As I closed my eyes, pleading with God to show me what He wanted me to do.

I saw in a vision, a huge black cloud that swayed backward and forward, swallowing everything in its path. There was a gigantic angel pushing the cloud away. I almost fell out of my seat. I asked God, "What does this have to do with what you want me to do"? I left church very frustrated and eventually settled down and forgot about the whole ordeal.

Needless to say, on March 1, 1997 at approximately 2:30 pm, An F-4 tornado hit the small town of Arkadelphia, Arkansas, killing six people and leaving mass destruction. I saw this monster in a vision before it came. I felt very sad and helpless afterwards. The next day I sat in sorrow and wrote my first poem, entitled "No Respect." Since then, I have written many poems from my visions, and dreams. Some of them have come true, others are left to the imagination, and the question, maybe in the future.

I pray that some of the dreams and visions will not come true because of the tragedies that I've seen. Tragedies bare heavy on my heart, mind, and soul. I've had reservations of sharing this with the world but God gave me these dreams and visions for a reason. I have dream and visions but I don't know when or where they will occur.

I want to encourage others who have special gifts similar to mine to share their experiences with the world. As a person, I'm usually sensitive and very serious. There are times when my thoughts shift, and become carefree, leading me to dwell on social issues that's humurous, and a bit nostalgic. I've expressed these feelings in many of my poems.

May your thoughts and imaginations be enlightened as you read, "Visions And Dreams Unveiled."

I want to dedicate this book to my late parents, Elmore & Pernella Wiley who inspired me to strive to be the best in life. I also give special thanks to my late Father-in-law, Rosboro Hendrix Sr. (papa) who was always very kind and humble.

About The Author

Sherrel Wiley Hendrix was born in Arkadelphia, Arkansas in a small community called Mill Creek. She is the second oldest of five siblings. She was raised on a farm, and treasures the value of hard work that was instilled in her by her parents. She attended Sparkman Public School, and later transferred to Arkadelphia Public Schools, where she graduated from high school in 1963. She received a B.S in Human Service from Hendrerson State University in 1996.

She is married to Rosboro Hendrix Jr., and the mother of four children, and nine grandchildren.

As a child, she wrote small plays, and pretend to produce them. She has always had visions and dreams that came true but kept them a secret fearing that others would see her as being odd. It is her desire to express her poetry to be understood by young and old. She writes about her visions, dreams, life experiences, tragedies, and inspirations to encourage other like herself to share their thoughts with the world.

# CONTENTS

# NO RESPECT

I saw you Twister in a vision before you came today.
We were warned but some people kept going their way.
While you were here, your roar was like a lion, going through the air,
up and down the streets, and all around.
You swallowed trees, homes, took people lives,
and scattered them on the ground.
You were big, black, and swirling around from the top to the ground.
You traumatized the town with your sound.
You could have been worse but God's angel quenched your thirst.
Because you came people of all races came together to help the other fellow.
Both Christians and sinners were spared.
Maybe God is telling us to get prepared.
God's angel stretched his strong white wings and told you to go,
and come back no more. You took your long tail and lifted it in the air,
and you dare not stare.

# WHO IS THIS MAN?

Early one morning about the break of day, God showed me a man by the way.

His statue was so magnificent, it left me speechless, and in a state of weakness.

The image was mirrored in my mind, lingering till endless time.

His white robe flowed as he stood holding a cross in his hands, smiling as he stands.

I pondered after I saw him, and asked myself" Who is this man?"

His face was  black as midnight, and had a certain aura.

His wooly black beard streamed half way his chest accenting his beautiful white vest.

I asked myself, who is this man?

I pondered as he looked into my eyes.

His smile was as if he was filled with mercy and grace.

I sensed that his appearance was all knowing and wise.

I ask myself, who is this man?

Each day, in my mind, I see his sparkling white teeth as he smiles at me.

I wonder, who was  that man?

I carry the cross in my heart that he held in his hands.

Wondering, who was that man?

His aura covers me with love like a dove flying above.

One day, God will reveal to me who that man is,

then I will fully understand.

# THE BLACK HOLE

Years of being trapped, the light I have not seen.

Darkness covers my soul, as I grow old.

Happiness, I have not taken.

From this black hole, I have not escaped,

wanting to get out before it's too late.

Each day, I struggle with good, and bad.

The bad seems a delight at times.

It over shadows my mind causing me to be unkind.

Some days, hope seems to be within my reach.

The glimpse of happiness is crushed when horrid thoughts over shadows,

sticking to me like a leech.

Good and evil forces encamp me as I struggle to defend my mind, and soul.

I ask the almighty for directions, waiting patiently for the truth to unfold in this smoky dark hole.

Looking above, seeing the light as it shines like pure gold,

and wondering, will I be free of this darkness that haunts, and taunts me day and night?.

Will I remain here till I'm old?

# ANGEL ENCOUNTER

I awaken out of a deep sleep on a warm summers' night.

A vibrant light glowed at the end of my bed.

The light filled the room like a full moon.

Within the light was an angel dressed in white.

Her appearance baffled my mind.

Her arms were opened wide.

At that very moment, I wanted to run, and hide.

As I looked at the glowing light,

it was as if I couldn't breathe any more.

I wanted to escape, but her statue covered the door.

I grasped for breath, I thought each breath would be the last.

I lay in bed motionless, I began to pray, and ask God to let me stay.

I closed my eyes, and God answered my prayer,

She dissipates into thin air bidding me farewell until another day.

# THE CORN FIELD

I saw miles and miles of corn.

Her stalks are green and tall, sitting in a bed of rich black soil.

As far as can be seen, miles and miles of corn.

The sun shines above the field overshadowing it like a dove ..

As far can be seen, miles and miles of dark green corn .

Her fullness is as a mother getting ready to give birth to her young.

The birds and bees gathers to feast on her leaves.

They swarm singing their song.

As far as can be seen miles and miles of dark green corn.

Her strength is in her stalks,

and her grandeur is eye catching as a hawk.

As far as can be seen, miles, and miles of rich, dark green corn.

# THE VOICE

One morning as I lay in bed, a powerful voice echoes into my ears and said,"
you don't belong to me."
I bow to God with a plea, to tell me what to believe.
God said, "The evil one is playing games with you,
trying to convince you to believe.
What better way to deceive"?
He's a trickster of his trade, and his lies are a facade.
His voice came upon me in disguise, because he's filled with lies.
He caught me off guard and pretends to be my Lord.
God gave me a spirit of discernment to recognize His voice.
I'll stay on guard and pray to my Lord.
Satan is on the prowl like the midnight owl.
He's there to seek and defile, because he's filled with lies.
He sits and waits like a snake charms his prey.
He enters in when there is a weak space.
He pretends to give me mercy and grace.
God's got my back and I'm armored for Satan's attack.
.

# FACES

My mind travels in many places, and I see many faces.

Fake smiles, frowns, happy faces,

expressions torn, and new ones to be born.

Faces that experience hard times.

Faces that have fine lines.

Faces that watches as you turn, and faces that are unconcerned.

Faces that are warm, faces that appears to be in a storm.

The image of faces in my mind, I wonder how many were mine.

# THE SNAKE

He creeps, and slithers on my skin trying to get in.

He pretends to be my friend.

He's under my skin trying to become a part of me.

I am struggling with all my might because I want him out of my sight.

He is a devil in disguise, cunning, and wise.

He is filled with deceitful lies.

He injects poison into my veins leaving me lame.

I detest the day he came.

He deceives me when I m weak, leaving me unable to speak.

He's just a creep!

He is a sly one.

He slithers down the tree in the cool of the day.

He watches as I walk his way.

He creeps in and claims his stake because he's a snake on the take.

I fell for his wrap and now I'm trapped.

My life is filled with the pains of labor with no favors.

I am under his spell, and it's like being in hell.

I disobeyed God, and ate the forbidden fruit.

I was put out of God's garden as a fugitive to labor in a land of thorns, and thistles.

The snake follows, slithering on his belly, striking my heel, trying to kill.

For my disobedience, I have to toil, and give birth in pain.

This life that I live is bitter as acid rain.

# IS IT REAL OR A DREAM?

Waking up practically in shock, drenched with sweat.
Tears are  streaming down my face.
I wonder if this experience was a dream,
or was it real, because it had no grace.
The sound of a gun shooting had me in a state of fear.
The experience was crystal clear.
My son was in the line of fire.
It dawned on me that he may die
I ask, "Is this a dream or is it real"?
I talked to my son, to see what was wrong.
He hesitates but finally tells the sad song.
The perpetrator pulls his gun.
No harm did he do to my son.
Instead, he decided to run.
The dream was a dream, and a reality.
God sends the dream as an alarm to
let the Mom and the son know,
that God protects His children from harm.

# BIG BUCKS

Luck! you may call it that, or the hand of God?

A long awaited dream has come true.

It was seen some time ago in clear view.

I got on my knees. I prayed without ceasing, fasting at times.

It seems  that I was losing my mind.

My face was bowed to the mother "Earth".

I bellowed out to God with words untold.

I dearly thank Him for riches, and fine gold

What will I do with the cash?

Will I be rash, and spend it on foolishness, and portray selfishness?

I remember what God has said in His word.

" It is more blessed to give than to receive". I must give back

to God and my blessing will be pressed down, and running over like clover.

God said it, that's it. I'll give to the ones that are in need.

This is how I will plant my seed.

# I NEED TIME

The Moon, sun, and stars are falling.
I'm in the mist of this calling.
The light is gone, and I'm alone.
The moon fell on the sun and it spattered like Mirth.
Darkness is all around. I can hear crackling sounds.
The stars are not here  any more.
Oh! I remember how beautiful they were before.
Why am I in this place alone?
Am I dreaming? Are these things that I see, real?
How I yearn to savor the past, maybe, I have lived to fast.
Oh God, I need time to make things right.
Please God give me time!
I pray thee with all my might.

# RUNNING

I am running and I'm searching.
Where can I go?
God, I really don't know.
Can I go north, south, east or west?
God, tell me which way is best!
Maybe, I can become superman, and fly
high in the sky. Maybe, I can hide in a box.
I know, I can dig a hole in the ground like a fox.
God, there's minutes before destruction.
Please give me some instructions!
I need to be in a safe place.
God, what would you do in my case?
Maybe, I can go to the moon.
Oh God! Oh God! Oh God! I see the light.
I must trust in you with all my might.
I can be safe in your arms,
and nothing can do me any harm.

# LEFT BEHIND

I was driven from my home. I roamed all day long.

An underground cave, I found.

I slept for a while, only to be awaken by shooting sounds.

On the run again, it seems that I can't win.

The evil one has filtrated the land.

It's more than I can stand.

Christians have been persecuted, and churches have been looted.

The evil ones gathered all the bibles and made a blazing fire.

They burned them and said that my God was a lie.

All the undecided ones mourned and cried.

I was left behind in this forsaken land.

How much more God can I stand?

I remember that I told the preacher a lie.

So much wrong that I've done to Gods' begotten son.

I never thought about asking God to forgive me.

I'm left in this forsaken land as you can see.

The enemy is closing in, and I'm on the run again.

It seem as if it will never end.

So many were forced to take the mark.

I refused, and now I'm a fugitive in the dark.

It's hard to resist, but I must persist.

All I have is God's words lingering in my heart, mind, and soul.

# TAKEN UP IN A CLOUD

I had a dream about my fathers well.

It was unique and had a very special bell.

When the other wells were dry, his was always spry.

One day, I was standing by his well.

The wind began to blow.

My body started flowing.

As the cloud came near, I was filled with fear.

I was lifted in the air by the swiftly winds

The man's face in the cloud was very clear.

The light around him was brighter than the setting sun.

His hair was as white as snow.

His garment had a special glow.

He called me by my name, and told me to take his hand.

In my mind, I didn't understand.

In a melodious voice that penetrates my heart, soul, and spirit.

God said," Don't be afraid,

I'm going to take you to a place where there is no pain or sorrow.

A place where time will stand still.

All of your dream and hopes will be fulfilled.

# MURDER ON HIS MIND

I was in a deep sleep.

Suddenly, I began to dream.

A man dressed in black was waiting in the back yard.

It was in the wee hours of the morn, as the dew fell on the lawn.

He smokes a joint and drinks his wine. He is angry.

He has murder on his mind.

Suddenly, a light has been turned on.

Through the open blinds, he sees her with his newborn son.

He is drunk with scorn and his mind is torn in the wee hours of the morn.

He suddenly takes out his sawed-off shot- gun.

He shoots, barely missing his newborn son.

The door was busted, and torn, glass spattered on the lawn.

I awaken from my dream and heard shots.

My family was in a state of shock because the door was shot.

The attacker cast his lots but God took over, and took us in His fold.

He left in a flash, but was slowed down in his drunken state.

He was caught by the police and met his fate.

# YOU WERE THERE

Through all my trials and tribulations,

You were there to give me consolation.

When I was burdened down, and didn't know what to do.

You told me to keep my eyes on Jesus

because He knows what you're going through.

You told me time after time that God has worked it out.

Just have faith, and never doubt.

It's been times in my life that I wanted to give up.

 You reminded me that God is sitting high and looking low.

He's taking me through these things to help me grow.

You were there telling me to be strong,

just keep your eyes on Jesus.

He'll be with you all day long,

even when you're wrong.

Through the years, you've stuck by me in my ups and downs.

You have steered me in the right direction,

and told me to look too God for protection.

Just hold on to God's unchanging hand.

With Him on your side, you'll be able to stand.

# THE VOICE OF A CHRISTIAN WOMAN IN TODAY'S WORLD

That soft and tender voice that's present with you every day.

It encounters hardship and pain,

but it reaches out with tenderness to let me  know that God is your gain.

That tender voice is filled with love, tenderness, kindness and compassion.

Although at times, it may seem a bit old fashion.

That tender voice builds, and mends relationships.

It sustains us when we're weak to get our bible and seek.

It calms us as newborn babes being song a sweet lullaby.

That tender voice has crossed many oceans, and seas.

It has supplied many needs.

That tender voice is crying out to you today.

It tells us to love each other with all our mind, soul, and heart.

Trust in God and don't depart.

That voice is quietly echoing in our ears

telling us to get down on our knees and pray that God will be in our hearts
    to stay.

It tells us to forgive our enemies as God has forgiven us.

For all the difficult situations, in God we must trust.

Meditate on His word, fast, and pray to not go astray.

Hold your gossiping tongue so God will keep you strong.

Keep your anger abreast because life is only a test.

# NO PAIN NO GAIN

Climbing the ladder of success is like

Putting a log through the eye of a needle.

You try this and that, and if you not

careful, you are out of whack.

It seems that I am working hard, and getting no where

I Just want to get on an airplane, and set to the air.

Climbing this ladder is distressing me. It is tiring me out.

The circumstances are pilling high, and time is running out.

I want to give up but I've got to climb this hill.

To give up will defeat God's will.

I must roll up my sleeves, and put on the breastplate of righteousness, and
believe that God will help me succeed.

I have to burn the midnight oil, and be willing to toil.

To succeed, I must remember to ask God for power, and strength to believe.

# REVIVE MY SOUL

Lord, when my heart becomes cold,

and bitterness encamps my soul.

Send me words to console!

Rekindle the joy within my soul!

Make me your servant,

and allow love to flow within my heart like pure gold.

Teach me your ways!

Touch my mind, heart, and soul in a mighty way!

Give me grace, and mercy each day!

Teach me to forgive others as God has forgiven me.

Guide my tongue as I speak,

and give me strength when I become weak!

Give me a spirit of discernment that I may stand firm in your word!

Hold me in your loving arms when I become absurd!

# I CAN WIN

Set your goals high, that you feel like reaching the sky.

Sometimes you may stumble.

Pick your self up, and don't grumble!

Life is full of ups and downs. Learn from your mistakes, and don't frown.

Just remember the race between the rabbit, and the tortoise.

The rabbit assumed that he would win.

He plays around until the end.

The tortoise set a goal.

He kept an even pace, and won the race.

When you're feeling low,

and you feel that you can't go on any more.

Remember the tortoise,

he set his goals high, and ended by reaching the sky.

# THE ANOINTING

When my troubles soar and I don't know which way to go. Lord, send your
anointing!

When the devil is attacking and I want to go packing. Lord, send your
anointing.

When I'm confused, and been misused. Lord, send your anointing.

I need you Lord every minute of the day to show me the way.

Lord, send your anointing!

It dawned on me the other day to get down on my knees and pray.

Oh Lord, send your anointing!

Let your anointing flow from the top of my head to the tip of my toes

like it ran down Arons' beard.

Lord, I need your anointing today to show me the way.

Oh Lord, send your anointing!

# THE HOURGLASS

Every second of the day that time passes away like the sand in the hourglass.

Time is running out without a doubt like the sand in the hourglass.

The sand in the hourglass is slowly pouring, and my heart is soaring.

Time is running out like the sand in the hourglass.

I ask God," what can I do to make a difference in this world. God said,

Tell your brothers and sisters not to stray, but to get down on their knees
and pray."

Time is running out like the sand in the hourglass.

People stop stealing, killing, and robbing your fellowman.

In God's own time, He's coming back like a thief in the night.

It's time to get it right.

Time is running out like the sand in the hourglass.

If you're caught with your work undone, too late,

You can't run.

Time is running out like the sand in the hourglass.

Parents teach your children the difference between right and wrong.

When you face God, you will not give an account of their wrong.

Time is running out like the sand in the hourglass.

Preachers preach what's in the bible,

live a godly life, and then people will see you as being reliable.

Time is running out like the sand in the hourglass.

# BRUISED

We have taken for granted that America is a safe place to live.

Never realizing that we may not have time to forgive.

On a beautiful, vibrant morning that was calm.

We didn't realize that there was a reason for alarm.

Quickly, the day turns gray, and shattered bodies lay.

America became spiritually, mentally, and physically torn.

Thousands never knew what hit them, leaving love ones to mourn.

People were literally going out of their minds.

Families crying, and asking," why," because their love ones can't be found.

Husbands have died, leaving babies yet to be born.

Children have been left homeless, and their hearts torn.

We have joined together for strength and comfort

to weather the storm, trusting in God to protect us from further harm.

Believing that the ones that committed this horrid act will be brought to justice.

Praying that peace will abide in this wonderful land,

and that our enemies will humble themselves in unity,

and become our fellowman.

# THE SLAIN LAMB

Our Savior was nailed on a cross.
It was a place of unflavored grace.
Some faithful ones followed along.
They were sad about what the leaders had done.
A crown of thorns was placed on His head,
piercing Him until blood stream from His face.
His back was torn from the lashes of the whip.
Soldiers gambled for His clothes. They laughed and sang an
Ungodly song. They did not  know that they will pay for their wrong.
On lookers mocked and spit on Him. Some said,"
If you're the Christ, Come form the cross and save your self."
He remained on the cross so our souls wouldn't be lost.
He will be coming back one day. Prepare now or pay the cost.
He will be coming back like a thief in the night.
Prepare each day so your soul will not be lost.

# SEARCHING FOR FORGIVENESS

I thirst for true forgiveness.

My heart lingers for the desire.

My mind hungers for the answers to be free.

I want to be free of

being a prisoner of an unforgiving heart.

My heart, soul, and mind thirst as if it's on fire.

A fire that burns deep within from all my unforgiving sins.

I want to be free as a bird that spreads his wings

and surges through the hurt and pain.

This unforgiving heart has a stain, that's without fame.

To find true forgiveness will be a treasure indeed.

I must seek Jesus, and get down on my knees.

I ask God for a pure heart, a heart that is patient and kind.

In my bible, the true treasure I've found.

# SEPARATION TIME IN THE CITY

Red, yellow, black, and white working together Monday through Saturday.

When Sunday comes, it's a different game.

It appears that we're not the same.

It's separation time in the city on the most sacred time of the week.

On Sunday our heart takes a separate path, as if a different God we seek.

Why does the color of our skin make a difference?

We all love, feel, have needs, hurt, and bleed.

When we die, will there be a back or white heaven or hell?

Look in the bible and it will tell.

Because I'm white, and rich in silver and gold,

Will God say," Brother, come in and take a special seat"?

Or because I'm black, and poor will He say," hit the door!"

Suppose all churches had to integrate.

Would we rant and rave, and say, before I comply, I'll go to my grave?

Each of us has to search our hearts

and ask God to give us a clean heart, and a new start.

We are all beautiful flowers in His garden, different colors, and size.

We all bleed the same color blood. We all hurt and have needs.

We will come face to face with the master

when our journey on this earth has ended.

We will give an account of the good and bad.

Get it right now, so our conscience will be clear,

and we'll meet God without fear.

# OOPS! OVER MY HEAD

Over my head in sin, no matter where I turn, I can't win.

No matter what the preacher say, I'm going to do it my way.

OOPS! OVER MY HEAD! What can I do?

I'm sinking low. I don't know which way to go.

I know my life has got to change.

I tossed and turned all night long, singing my sad song.

Oh Lord! What can I do to straighten up my

Act, and get my life back on track?

OOPS! OVER MY HEAD, What can I do?

I looked to the left, there was something standing over my head.

I said," Good God almighty, Am I living or dead?

I looked to the right, there was a light shinning bright that almost knocked
     to the floor.

There was a man standing there with his arms wide open,

telling me there's going to be a brighter day,

just keep the faith, and He'll show me the way.

OOPS! OVER MY HEAD! What can I do?

# CONFUSED

Tall, dark and handsome is my name.

Education is not my game.

Each day, frustration, and anger I feel.

My happiness it steals, makes me want to kill.

Gang banging is my reputation.

Profanity is my conversation.

I ask myself, why do I feel angry?

My father left me when I was small.

I didn't get to know him at all.

My mother worked two jobs to give me food, shelter, and clothing.

I craved love, respect, and fellowship.

My momma died last year, since then, I've been living in constant fear,

watching my back, and all like that.

Tonight, I lay in my mommas' bed.

I can hear her voice echoing inside of me.

Son, go back to school, and follow the golden rule.

If you want companionship, join a church, and fellowship.

Give love, and respect to all mankind.

In Gods' eyes this is a good sign.

# SWEET TUNES OF FREEDOM

Freedom is ringing like a bell, sweeter than the sound of a harp.

Ringing here, there, and everywhere.

My mind, heart, and, soul is in tune to the sweet tunes of freedom.

I heard Gods voice saying,

come hither my child through the open door,

and step up to the first floor.

Come hither to the enchanting, and everlasting light.

There is a special delight.

I have prepared a place where the chains of backstabbing,

lying, stealing, sickness, and dying have been defeated.

Come hither my child to a special feast.

Come hither my child to a land of milk and honey.

There, you don't have to worry about money.

I'll give you wings like a dove to soar from above.

Sweet tunes of freedom my child in a land where you'll never grow old.

Come hither my child and sing praises of freedom.

Come hither my child and dance to the tunes of sweet freedom.

Sweet tunes of freedom of my Lord and Savior, Jesus Christ.

I'll be standing somewhere around His throne, where age and time will stand
    still.

In that land, my soul, and spirit will be fulfilled.

# GET THIS STUFF OUT OF THE CHURCH!

I know some people think that I'm bold,

but I've have a story and it must be told.

Some of our churches have gone worldly

with tradition and no mission.

Instead of a vision, it's a collision.

Jesus said, " Where there is no vision the people perish."

People lets get together and get this stuff out of the church.

Deacons and Trustees are calling someone else wife honey,

and giving them their money.

Certain ladies come in late on Sunday mornings so they can be seen in their best attire,

thinking they're on fire with all kinds of wild desire.

People lets get together and get this stuff out of the church.

Preachers are watching the young ladies from their heads to their toes,

and can spot all the pretty ones on each row.

People lets get together and get this stuff out of the church.

Some people think that our churches are a social click,

and tell some to get back quick.

People lets get together and get this stuff out of the church.

All this stuff about my church is bigger and better than yours.

When you see certain people coming, you close the doors.

People lets get together and get this stuff out of the church.

Jesus said, "I'm coming back like a thief in the night."

He's going to be awesome and out of sight.

While you have time, lets get it right.

People lets get together and get this stuff out of the church.

# CAMOUFLAGE

I am hiding behind a smile.
Pretending for a while...
I feel like an abandoned child.
I can no longer pretend.
I can't let anyone inside.
My life is filled with lies.
Covering the hurt and pain...
I leave no room for fame.
The stench of war is inside.
It nags my mind, heart, and spirit.
Daily, I'm reminded that I have nothing to gain but pain.
Loneness impounds, echoing within.
It tears my mind and spirit apart.
I am crying inside for someone to rescue me.
Tears of sadness is locked inside.
I can't trust anyone nor can I confide.
No one must see or hear my cries.
Thoughts of ending it, but that's not the way.
I'm praying tomorrow will be a better day.
I pray that God will step in and show me the way.

# HIS WILL

He gently whispers into my ear, a melodious voice that flows like milk and
   honey.

His instructions were plain, and clear. I had other things on my mind.

I ran here and there. I said, "not today, maybe another time".

I partied all night long, and I sang an ungodly song.

There were perverted words coming from my tongue.

I didn't care about doing wrong.

One morning as I was coming off of one of my usual highs.

A gentle, melodious voice flowed into my ears once again.

It purged my heart, and bought me to my knees.

At that very moment, I repented with a plea.

With tears streaming down my face,

I ask God for mercy and grace.

He kindly adhered to my request.

I promised Him that very day,

I would give Him my best.

# IN THE MIDST

I was sitting in this congregation, and

I heard a gentleman say," I could have been dead and sleeping in my grave, but

I thank God that I am alive".

Another man sitting on the front seat, stood up, and grabbed the minister by the hand.

He said, "I was sitting here filled with sorrow with no hope for tomorrow.

The Holy Spirit came upon me and moved my sorrow.

I thank God for restoring my hope for tomorrow."

An old gentleman in the far corner stood up and began to

Shout, "to God be the glory, I'm here to tell the story."

A young man in a wheel chair came rolling down the aisles singing.

The whole story has not been told.

The streets in heaven are paved with gold.

There's a tree that's filled with healing leaves.

You are foolish if you don't believe.

# THE TONGUE

The tongue can tame a lion or it can send fury through the winds.

It can throw you in a rage or transcend melodious sounds.

It has mounted many wars, and killed many relationships.

The tongue makes twists, and turns,

and can bellow out happiness, and delight.

It can be as a pink tornado, and brew a storm that's out of sight.

The tongue can send negative vibes that affect people lives.

The tongue sings sweet songs of mercy, and grace.

It can send the roar of thunder with a sour taste.

The tongue dumps its waste on others each day.

Sometime we have to exhale,

and tell the tongue to take a break.

Please empty the waste for peace sakes!

# STICKS AND STONES

Sticks and stones may break my bones, but the word of

God will put me back together again.

Hey now! I said, "sticks and stones may break my bones but the word of God
will put me back together again." Hey Now!

His word will hold me, console me, soothe me, and feed me.

Hey now! "I said sticks and stones may break my bones,

but the word of God will put me back together again." Hey Now!

You can stone me, break me, shake me, forsake me,

but the word of God will put me back together again, Hey Now!

I said sticks and stones may break my bones,

but the word of God will put me back together again. Hey Now!

# GOD AWESOME POWER

When I think about God's grace and how He saved the human race.

I feel like shouting, and never to doubt Him.

He was at a wedding one night, and oh! It was out of sight.

He changed water into wine, and he did it on time.

With a clap of his hands, He healed the sick,

made the crippled walk, and the dumb to talk.

There is no greater power that you can find,

and its' been around since the beginning of time.

With a blink of His eyes, he calms your fears, and dries your tears.

He told Moses to stretch out his rod,

and the Red sea came apart.

There is no greater power that you can find, and its' been around since the
   beginning of time.

Gods' power is awesome, and He helps those that are in need.

I thank Him for doing His fathers' will.

On the cross, He stood still.

There is no greater power you can find, and

Its' been around since the beginning of time.

# GIVE THANKS

For every day of life that God has given you...Give Thanks

For the things He has brought you through... Give Thanks

For dying on the cross for our sins, and the broken hearts He mends... Give Thanks

For the fresh air that we breathe and the wind that scatters the leaves...Give Thanks

For health and strength, and for His son He sent... Give Thanks

For protecting us as we sleep,

and His grace and mercy to keep...Give Thanks

For the sun that shines, and good, and bad times... Give Thanks

For deliverance of jealously, hate, and anger... Give Thanks

For putting a bridle on our tongues so we will not do wrong... Give Thanks

God has said in His word, "In everything give thanks."

This is the will of Christ Jesus concerning you.

# MY MAN AND YOURS TOO

I have a passion to know his will and ways.
I longed to be with Him for the rest of my days.
I can't wait to praise and worship Him.
I want to be in His presence as I lay.
I want to be with Him each minute of the day.
I recognize Him as being" Lord of Lords" and
King of Kings." I honor him as I pray.
I love Him with all of my heart, soul, and mind.
I know He will be my man till the end of time.
I know that He's filled with mercy and grace.
I want to seek Him each day of my life.
I know that someday I'll meet Him face to face.
Until then, I'll take a pinch of His faith.
I'll dine on His wisdom, and patiently wait.

# A GOD CHASER

I yearn to know Him better.
His words are a beautiful written letter.
He's mine all mine.
I can talk to Him at any time.
He is constantly on my mind.
His love is genuine as gold.
He is the best love story that's ever been told.
I can trust him with my deep dark secrets.
He keeps them in a special place.
He treats them with love and grace.
He's there to forgive me when I'm wrong.
He stands by my side and tells me to be strong.
He's more valuable than silver or gold.
He stands by me when I need to be bold.
He is within me, consoling me, and protecting me.
He's like no other friend.
He'll be with me until the end.

# HE'S WORTHY UP IN HERE

I'm going to praise God up in here.

He's worthy up in here. He's worthy up in here.

I'm going to praise Him while I can because He's worthy up in here.

When depression comes on me, and I can't see my way through.

I'll get on bended knees, and look up to Him.

That's the way it's going to be.

He's worthy up in here. He's worthy up in here.

# GOING TO PRAISE HIM UP IN HERE

When my peers tell me to do wrong,

I'm going to sing the same old song.

That's the way it's going to be.

I'm going to praise Him up in here.

When they look at me strange because I'm praising God's name.

That's the way it's going to be. I'm going to praise Him up in here.

He's worthy to be praised.

I'm not looking for fame, just want to praise God's name.

Just want to lift up holy hands, and praise Him while I can.

That's the way it's going to be.

Going to praise Him up in here, up in here.

# IN HIS COURTYARD

Come hither my beloved and gather in my courtyard.

Bow to me my beloved! I am your Lord.

I made you in my image. Every part of you

I know, even to the inner core.

I know your inner thoughts, and desires.

In your heart, my word is to reside.

With the slain blood of my son, I saved you.

You are my beloved child, and I love you with all my heart.

Depend, and lean on me for my love will never depart.

# FARM LIFE

Duties, duties, duties, I don't have enough time during the day to do the
    chores.

I have to get up early or mother will whip my booty.

I've got to milk the cows, and chop the wood.

I have no time for idleness.

I'm working like I should.

I am planting the seeds in the garden, and keeping a steady pace.

Mother is peeping through the crack of the door.

I don't want a whipping any more.

The chickens are in the barn feasting on corn.

They don't know when they become fat their necks will be torn.

I got the old bucket and footstool to milk old Betsy.

She greets me with delight because her bags are tight.

It seems old Betsy was relieved.

So much milk, I could hardly believe.

Picking cotton in the field,

and longing for the sun to go down.

We're anxious for Mom to ring the supper bell.

We soon  heard the tone of the bell.

Our feet made dents into the ground.

We raced our way to our little white house,

running faster than a mouse.

We hurriedly, and sat at the table to eat moms black eyed peas,

mash potatoes and hot apple pie.

Oh! our tummies were relieved.

We gave mom a big hug.

She tucked us in bed as tight as a bug.

We thanked the Lord for our souls to keep, and quickly fell asleep.

# WASHING IN THE 50'S

I drew bucket after bucket of water from the well.

I filled the old black wash pot until it was filled to the brim.

I was tired as can be as you can tell.

I just want to sit a spell. Mother said," I can't stop."

Sister watching, and saying," if you stop, I will tell."

The fire around the old black wash pot is blazing hot.

The water is boiling to the top.

I filled the old squeaky washing machine,

and watched as it churned up and down, and around.

I was tired as could be, but I couldn't stop.

I put the clothes in the ringer, and they slithered through like a snake,

being careful not to make a mistake.

Rinsing the clothes in tubs of water, again and again…

It seems as if washing will never end.

The day is almost gone.

The winter breeze is whistling her tone.

I have pinned the clothes on the line.

Finishing this task is on my mind.

The clothes swing as the cold wind blows.

They quickly freeze in the evening breeze.

It's almost dark, and the washing is done.

I watched the clothes glitter against the evening sun.

I lie and wait for another day, and more chores to be done.

# FATHER TO SON

Boy! why are you sitting in that chair brewing trouble?

You're causing dissention trying to get attention.

Boy! I told you to read that book,

and don't give me that pitiful look.

Boy! You're going to need your high school diploma.

Some jobs are going to require a college education.

Boy! You got to prepare yourself for all situations.

Boy! Get that pitiful look off your face!

Pace your self in that room and fetch your books!

When you come out, get the frowns out your face.

You need to have a pleasant look.

I want you to do your math like it's a craft.

Conjugate those verbs like you drive your car in a curb.

Spell those words as fast as a bird flying in the sky.

It'll be all right if you make a mistake, just try!

I didn't lean the golden rule.

Don't be an uneducated fool,

study your lesson, and stay in school.

# THOUGHTS

What if my thoughts were open to the world?

Would I be sentenced to jail or hell?

Many thoughts have entered my mind: laughter, kindness, love, and joy.

I have had thoughts of revenge, malice, and hate as well.

Thoughts, if seen with the naked eye would shatter the mind until the end of time.

Thoughts of hatred to another… thoughts, you wouldn't tell your mother.

Evil thoughts that lie dormant within the mind seemingly do no harm.

When in action, it enrages the mind like a storm.

Thoughts of good and evil are in battle at all times.

Evil thoughts leave the mind empty and bare.

Thought of peace and love is like the splendor of a dove that's filled with love.

# JACK LEG PREACHER

Jack Leg Preacher is what my daddy called him.

He comes to our door every Sunday after church.

He tips his hat, and uses our house like a door matt.

Saying," good afternoon maim."

At the same time, He peeps to see what on the kitchen table.

Momma said," sit another plate for the Reverend."

I knew what would happen when he started to eat.

He said," girly, pass me the meat!" Not one, but six pieces did he eat.

We all sat with our mouths wide open.

He said, "Girly, this chicken show is good."

Momma chuckled like I knew she would.

In a voice that's nice and all. She said," help yourself Reverend."

The Reverend sat a spell and slept as well.

Daddy came home and saw that all the chicken was gone.

With his gun by his side, and his mouth open wide.

All he could say was, " Jack Leg Preacher"

# LIFE'S JOURNEY

While traveling through life, I've wondered why time is short.

Before you know it, the days and years are gone, and you're left alone.

As I look back, and I remember being a toddler, young adult and middle age.

Old age stares at me without grace.

As I look in the mirror, I see a wrinkle here, and there.

Reminiscing of the days when I was so fair, with a coke bottle figure, and
long black hair.

I had a strut in my walk, and stares as I talk.

Now there is gray in my hair, and I'm not as fair.

The strut is gone.

Uncle author has set in, and liniment is my friend.

At times, I yearn that I could turn back the clock.

I want to become young and vivacious again.

I have to accept the fact that time cannot reverse itself,

 nor can it stand still.

It is the will of my heavenly father that I accept old age with grace, and
dignity.

I am thankful to go through life's journey, and enjoy

My children, grand's, family, and friends.

In the midst of it all, I am thankful that I found Jesus.

He will be with me till the end.

# VANISHING HEARTS

The glow is fading like the sunset.

My heart aches as the sequel ends.

In some ways, I want to pretend that love is abreast.

Two hearts started in the same direction.

Somewhere in the bustle of every day life, hearts swayed.

They took a different path.

Our hearts have grown cold to the whims of the each others needs.

They are trying to fulfill empty deeds.

One heart pretends that the love has been savored.

The other regrets and broods over wasted tears, and years.

One heart is filled with emotions, and desires love.

It has vanished as if it has never been.

One still pretends, maybe until the bitter end.

# TO BE LOVED

We share, and care.

We have a special smile that lingers for a while.

We touch each other with a special touch that means so much.

He knows that I am his queen and he is my king.

We know that whatever situation arises, our

Love will endure for sure.

He thinks of my needs before his.

We know that it is our Heavenly Fathers' will.

We both know that God's begotten son has put us together.

We know that our love will endure forever.

# IN HIS COURTYARD

Come hither my beloved and gather in
My courtyard. Bow to me my beloved for
I am your Lord.
I made you in my image. Every part of you
I know, even to the inner core.
I know your inner thoughts, and desires.
In your heart, my word is to reside.
With the slain blood of my son, I saved you.
I will be with you in all your ups and downs.
You are my beloved child, and I love you with all my heart.
Depend and lean on me, and my love will not depart.

# MY BELOVED

I'll set you on a pedestal besides me for the world to see.

My beloved is mine and I'm hers.

Thou art my love till time on earth ends.

My beloved, my friend is as a pillar of fine gold.

Her lips are sweeter than wine.

Her voice is as calm as a lamb.

She lays her head on my shoulder as I whisper songs of love into her ear.

Her body touches mine, and we are as one in mind, heart, spirit, and soul.

My beloved, my friend, you are more precious than the finest gold.

Our love is the best love story that's ever been told.

# LOVE LEFT ME

Lovers that were in love, but as time passed,

love became tainted with selfishness.

The bliss shifted to bitterness.

Love was lost like a sinking ship trying to float on water.

Oh love! How I desire thee. How can I take away the bitterness?

My heart yearns for your return.

You have left me alone. Oh Love! how I moan.

I lay awake at night hoping that you'll return.

Oh Love! how my heart yearn.

My heart is bruised.

My thoughts are tainted with hopelessness, and I feel misused.

How can I go on? Will you ever return? Oh! Love how my heart yearn.

I want to pretend that this nightmare is a dream.

When I awaken love will be by my side.

I can take this nightmare and toss it in the sea of forgetfulness.

I'll say to love, "you have not forsaken me".

# SHE LOVES ME SHE LOVES ME NOT

When she loves, and honors him and greets him with a kiss...

Will he tenderly embrace her, and give her a kiss?

or say," that's what she's suppose to do."

For her very kind deeds, will he supply her needs?

When she listens to his woes.

She messages him from his head to his toe.

Will he look into her eyes and say, much obliged or will he say, it's late, I'm
tired.

# WHEN SHE'S HAD A HARD DAY.

Will he take up the slack or greet her with words of attack?

Will he listen to her woes, or will he say, fix my plate, ignore her,

and leave the room on his tipsy toes.

Is he caring, considerate, and kind?

Or is he selfish, dominating,

and drives you out of your mind?

Will you love him as a child of God?

Or, will you kick him to the curb with harsh words?

# A NEW DAY

As the sun peeks through the clouds,

yesterday slowly passes away.

The stars glow as the sun slowly disappears.

The sky waits, as the new day unfolds.

Red, brown, and yellow leaves scatters as the wind blows.

The squirrels leap from tree to tree.

What a spectacular sight to see!

Birds are flying and chirping.

They gather food for their young, singing their song.

The sound of trucks, and cars romping up and down the road.

Some are carrying a heavy load.

The coffee is brewing in the kitchen,

reminding me of days of old.

I will cherish this day in my heart forever..

I patiently wait to see the new day unfolds.

# SEEDS OF JOY

Invisible to the naked eye,
I'm slowly beginning to spry.
I started out very small.
On the way out I may need an overhaul.
For a while, here I must stay.
Soon I'll have legs to stand, and a brain to help me plan.
I'll make changes week by week. Soon, I'll be able to speak.
I'll have to make a big turn for my arrival.
This is necessary for my survival.
My room is consumed with red, yellow, and blue balloons.
I know that I will play with them soon.
I look forward to that blessed day when I can say in a loud cry.
Hey! Mom and Dad, I'm here, and I'm okay.

# RAINDROPS

Raindrops fall one by one.

So many, you can't count them all.

Sometimes they fall ten feet tall.

Raindrops fall like London Bridges is falling down.

Cities and towns are sometimes devastated.

Raindrops cause rivers to flow, and flowers to grow.

Raindrops rain tears in our lives.

Raindrops cause heartache and pain.

Broken hearts are torn, but joy comes in the morn.

Tiny raindrops water the tiny seeds.

They can grow at great speed.

Tiny raindrops beat against my windowpane.

It puts me in a relaxed, and sleepy mood.

I leap with joy because they came.

# THE MAGNOLIA

Her flowers are luscious, and in full bloom.
She stands out like a full moon.
Her sweet fragrance soothes the soul like days of ole.
Many winds have brushed against and through her,
but she yet stands.
God has protected her with His powerful hands.
She has withstood pain, rejection, devastation,
and many wars in all nations.
Storms have echoed through her mighty limbs.
She has withstood the whims.
Her leaves scatter as the lashing wind blow.
Her flowers gracefully fall beneath the bow.
Her beauty remains in tact with a brilliant glow.
Her fragrance soothes many hearts, and souls.
She stands tall in statue and strength.
Her flowers are beautiful, and has a vibrant sent.

# CAPTURED MOMENTS

Captured moments that dwells in my soul, stolen while taken on a stroll.

The glair of the sun against my face.

I am captivated by the beauty of nature as I pace.

The smell of daffodils as I stroll is more precious than gold.

Spring is in the air, and adoration is in my heart as I stare.

The squirrels jump from limb to limb, gathering food for their young.

The birds are chirping and playing, singing their song.

The children are laughing and playing, swinging high,

and low seeing how fast they can go.

The day will pass away.

The captured moments will remain in my heart to stay.

# RAY OF SUNSHINE

If I were a sunflower.
I would brighten the world.
With my long green stems,
I would write a hymn.
A hymn that would give hope
to sadness, and wipe out all
madness.
I would bravely walk the
streets, and be a friend to
every one I meet.
I would feed the hungry
and be a friend to the
lonely.
Having peace, joy, and love,
I would give praises to God above.
With a smile on my sun shinny face,
I would give hope to the human race.

# WHO LET THE DEVIL OUT?

Who let the devil out? Hoot, Hoot

Who let the devil out? Hoot, Hoot…

He's cunning and sneaky, and a little bit freaky.

He sneaks in your mind and occupy your time.

Who let the devil out? Hoot, Hoot…

Who let the devil out? Hoot, Hoot…

He moves and he groves, and he eventually rules.

Who let the devil out? Hoot, Hoot…

Who let the devil out? Hoot, Hoot…

If you let him in he'll tell you wrong is right.

When you've messed up and out of luck…

He'll tell you not to be uptight.

Who let the devil out? Hoot, Hoot

Who let the devil out? Hoot, Hoot

He travels to and fro, high and low.

Looking to see whom he can devour…

It makes no difference if you're rich or poor.

Who let the devil out? Hoot, Hoot…

Who let the devil out? Hoot, Hoot…

He's constantly on the prowl.

He enters the mind until it's defiled.

Who let the devil out? Hoot, Hoot…

Who let the devil out? Hoot, Hoot…

# ENTICEMENT

You delight me, showing me how good life can be.

You invigorate my soul, showing me all your fine gold.

You are asking me to only serve you.

To give up the true and living God.

You told me that you would give me the desires of my heart.

Just serve only you. Oh Lord! what shall I do?

The voice inside hesitates.

What should I tell this man that's telling me all these things?

He wears diamond rings and looks like a king.

I'm tempted to give in but it's something about this man that I don't understand.

He wants my soul and he promises me gold.

I pondered to myself, how will it profit me to lose my soul for a token of gold?

Oh God! What should I do?

The voice inside said," All that shines is surly not gold."

His words are cunning, but I better keep running.

He may be stunning, but I better keep running.

Turn him down and he will not stick around.

If you give in, you surly will not win.

God is the captain of my soul.

He has promised me the desires of my heart.

His word will not depart.

# HYPOCRITE

Typical family man, goes to church, character seems impeccable.

But, when I see him sneaking out late on Saturday night,

going to bars, and strip joints, incognito,

my mind goes into a spin, knowing that he has sinned.

He takes the women of the night to sleazy motels.

He dines them with fine wine, thinking no one will see or tell.

It's something about him that doesn't jell.

He comes to church on Sunday morning,

praying to the almighty,

shouting all over the church, acting as if his soul with God is well.

As soon as he knows someone has strayed from God,

he's right there to accuse, and charge.

He leaves church with his chest stuck out,

thinking he's done a great deed,

not looking at himself as breaking Gods' creed.

He tells others problems to everyone he meets,

and scatters their business in the street.

Sir, I want to inform you that there is a scripture in the bible that

says," Clear the log in your eyes first,

and bridle the tongue so you want be cursed."

# CUNNING LIES

Savior the times when there's joy in your life.

The devil sees your joy,

and tries to destroy it like a child frustrated with a toy.

He tells you lies that seem right.

He'll cause you to be restless throughout the night.

Oh Lucifer! You're so cunning and evil, sneaking through the cracks,

and crevices of people lives, pushing like a pack of flies.

You come in many disguises, trying to enter in.

When you see you can't win, you back off like a dog that has been whipped,

with his tail between his hind legs.

You regroup and start turmoil in weak minds making them unkind.

You travel to and fro seeking whom you can devour.

Your evilness will end one day.

There will come a day when you will pay.

# EXPOSED

Lies are mounting high, stacked to the ceiling, climbing to the sky.

The disguise has been blown. I feel pressure, and frustration.

It's difficult to remain calm. I am faced with this difficult storm.

The veil has been torn.

My power has been diffused, feeling abandoned, and abused.

Being exposed has tinged me from within.

These things, I must face, and not pretend.

The greed of money and power taints my thoughts because I was caught.

Trust has been tainted with lies, breaking family ties.

My spirit and mind strays, being haunted night,

and day. No comfort as I lay.

# A SET UP

It's a demonic spirit that spreads like a disease. Stop It Please!

God gave us life and it's to be treasured,

not thrown away in a flash of madness, as insane as the killing of Cane.

Satan deceives us into breaking rules, playing us as fools.

He gets into the minds of men, women, boys, and girls,

and tells them to kill at will, kill until your desire is fulfilled.

After you have snorted cocaine until your brains have fried,

hopefully you will have enough brains left to realize that he has lied.

You played into his hands.

He used and abused you. Now your body is a shell.

He's leaving you to find another soul to sit a spell.

# LOST IN THE CRACKS

Young, handsome and bold, wearing saggy pants, and fine gold.

Wrapping to the latest music not missing a beat.

Going to school staying out of his seat.

Focusing on the latest styles, driving the teacher, and his parents wild.

Every time I turn around, he's in the principal's office for this and that,

snapping and talking back.

He comes to school to socialize.

He hasn't picked up a book in a while.

He's falling though the cracks

plus he doesn't know how to act.

How do I reach him to teach him skills, and facts?

He doesn't want to listen to what I say.

He tells me he'll learn this stuff another day.

He wants to do things his way.

Banging, and wrapping to the latest beat,

will not stay in his seat.

He thinks he's cool.

He fails to realize that if he does not learn to read,

he'll become an uneducated fool.

# A WATCH DOG

Eyes are on me, piercing my inner soul.

Purging my thought, watching everything that I do or say.

Waiting for me to make a mistake,

and to say that I'm a fake.

Eyes are on me watching like a watchdog,

stalking my every move.

Can't hide, I have to abide.

Eyes are on me,

waiting with anticipation for me to fall into divers den.

Sneaky, piercing eyes filled with gossiping lies.

Eyes are on me when I meditate,

watching when I don't relate.

I can't escape even at my darkest moment.

Those eyes are like a watchdog getting ready to catch his prey.

Watching and waiting with no hesitation, and with full anticipation.

# A SLAUGHTERED GENERATION

A tiny seed was growing inside.

An evil idea entered my mind.

That deceiver convinces me that my body belongs to me,

as he did Eve.

He was so convincing that I believed.

I slaughtered the seed, and tossed it aside like a weed.

That deceiver told me a pack of lies, and now the blood is on my hands.

God! This craziness is more than I can stand.

A generation of people killed, my people!

How can I seek forgiveness from this tiny, innocent seed?

Oh God, how my heart bleed!

A part of me is destroyed, and nothing can make it right.

The guilt haunts, and taunts me day, and night.

I wonder if God will forgive me or tell me to get out of His sight.

One day, I'll come face to face with those tiny seeds.

I am pleading with God on bended knees to forgive me of these sinful deeds.

# LITTLE THINGS COUNT

In memory of Rosboro Hendrix Sr.

You had a special way that made my day,

and complimentary things to say.

When I was feeling sad, your kindness made me glad.

The way in which you said," thank you," made me feel brand new.

You sprinkle cheer in the community

with your kind deeds sharing with those in need.

You will always be loved by your family,

and talked about so kindly.

I know that you are looking down on the

great grandchildren that were born after you were gone.

I want you to know that we have planted your kindness in their hearts.

They will grow up knowing that their great papa gave them a great start.

# THIS MAN FROM GOD

Dedicated to Rev. C. D. Hood

After a lot of prayer, and supplication.

God sent this man to us, and he came without a fuss.

Because he came, our lives have changed.

I want to tell you about this man that is a part of Gods' plan.

Kindness, love, joy, and peace is in his heart.

God put it there from the start.

He prayed for patience. God gave it to him and a revelation.

When he stumbles, God gives him strength to carry on, and not to grumble.

His footsteps are marked with humbleness, and meekness.

Like an eagle, he shows no weakness.

This man that stands tall, God will not allow him to fall.

Can't you see that this man is a part of God's plan?

# SIXTY YEARS OF BLISS
(In Memory of My parents)

Well old lady, you have touched my heart.

God told me from the beginning that we would never part.

I must admit that this journey has been long, a little weary, and teary.

I want you to know the day I ask you to marry me, I was as nervous as a bee.

I got down on my knees and ask God to help me.

I had a little talk with God and I said to Him," I have found the most beautiful girl in the world.

God, I want this lady to be my wife. To be with me for the rest of my life."

God told me that she was the one, and that I was in store for a lot of fun.

I put on the full armor of God years ago.

I knew those pitfall were going to knock on my door.

I put God's word in my heart to ensure me to walk, talk, to think right, and not to fight.

God told me if I would follow His instructions, everything, will be okay.

I can say to you that you're sweeter than a honeybee.

You're the sugar in my tea, and the cream in my coffee.

God has blessed us with a love  that is longer than the deepest sea.

# LETS BREAK IT DOWN
Dedicated to the Alternative Education

Class today we are going to do something new.

Sly, take it to the top and don't let it drop!

Listen to me:

Art thou my Romeo? you are my home-o, a kind soul in my portfolio, Oh Romeo!

Lets break it down now. Ah break it down now.

You're my home-o, a kind soul in my portfolio, Oh Rome-o! Ah break it down now.

Let's break it down now.

Oh Juliet, my love beget from a different set.

My heart skips a beat with a leap. My Juliet, ah Juliet. lets break it down now,

break it down now.

Oh Rome-o! call me your love from above like a dove. Oh Rome-o,

the orchard walls are high, and tall.

Oh Juliet, you are my love and all. I hear your beacon call.

Come to me my love beget from a different set. Don't fret. You are my

love beget.

Lets break it down now , ah break it down now.

Oh Rome-o, my Rome-o, I love you with all my heart, mind, and soul. I'll run high and low.

I'll be with you where ever you go, through the wind,, and rain, and heart ache and pain.

Oh Rome-o, My Rome-o let's break it down now. Ah break it down now.

# IT'S CHRISTMAS TIME IN THE CITY

Lights shinning brightly everywhere I go.

Reminding me that it's Christmas time in the city.

Santa rings his bell, taking a list from all the boys, and girls.

It's Christmas time in the city as you can tell.

The carolers sing Christmas cheer,

up and down the streets to every one they meet.

It's Christmas time in the city as you can tell.

I'm bringing chimes of cheer to you on this precious day.

I wish each of you A Merry Christmas, and a Happy New Year as well..

It's Christmas time in the city as you can tell.

# HE'S A KING

Sweet baby Jesus, so humble He lay,

surrounded by animals, and a heaping pile of hay.

The profits told of His birth long before this day.

A star sets high in the sky to lead the wise men to the city where He lay.

So humble, meek, and mild.

Sweet, baby Jesus, Joseph and Mary's beautiful child.

# A CHRISTMAS PRAYER

Let happiness reign in all nations.

Let peace prevail among all people.

Let love be the main station.

Let broken relationships mend.

Let friendships reach greater heights.

Let fellowship become their delight.

Let the different races come together, and share a common bond.

Let all celebrate the birth of God's begotten son.

Let negative vibes be forever gone.

Let happiness reach a greater tone.

Let families reign in unity to benefit the welfare of the community.

Let friendships grow, and spread to all nations like a bountiful river flows.

Let us share with those that are less fortunate as God has asked, for this is
our task.

Let hunger become a figment of the past.

Let plenty for all prevail at last.

Let our love for God reach from breast to breast.

In the end, when it's all said and done,

we'll all meet in that great land and be His guest.

# ABOUT THE AUTHOR

Sherrel Wiley Hendrix was born in Arkadelphia, Arkansas in a small community called Mill creek. She is the second oldest of five siblings. She was raised on a farm. She treasures the value of hard work that was instilled in her by her parents. She attended Sparkman Public School, and later transferred to Arkadelphia Public Schools. She received a B.S in Human Service from Hendrerson State University.

She is married to Rosboro Hendrix Jr., and the mother of four children, and nine grandchildren.

As a child, she would write small plays, and pretend to produce them. She has always had visions and dreams that came true but kept them a secret fearing that others would see her as being odd. It is her desire to express her poetry to be understood by young and old. She writes about her visions, dreams, life experiences, tragedies, and inspirations to encourage other like herself to share their thoughts with the world.